GRIEF

A Survivor's Guide for Grief

By John S. Partilla

Comments by Professionals:

"After 40 years in the field, I can finally hand my clients a tool rather than just hold their hand in speechless empathy."
Paul A. Grzybowski LCSW, BCD, MSW, ACSW Clinical Director, Craig Academy

"This beautiful book is long overdue. Grieving can finally be seen in full color with encouragements to personalize it with your own stories, feelings and memories. A must for all who are grieving!"
Lulu Orr, R.N. Executive Director, Good Grief Center for Bereavement Support

"I found your book loaded with heartfelt truisms which I think should be very helpful to grieving people. I feel that the material is appropriate for any given point in the grieving process, because we change so often in where we are with our grief, the book can be read again and again."
Sandy Conaway, Grief and Loss Counselor

To order additional copies of this book, contact:
Xlibris
844-714-8691
www.Xlibris.com
Orders@Xlibris.com
619400

J Dawg

Thank you for always running
in front and looking back
to see if I was okay.
Thank you for being my companion.
Thank you for keeping
me warm at night.
Thank you for never complaining.
Thank you most of all for
being in my life and always
being there for me.
You were my best friend.
I will see you again.

Ian and J-Dawg

GRIEF SUCKS

A book for every backpack, purse or briefcase.

A book for every coffee table.

A book needed in every school library.

A book for every family.

A book for giving and keeping.

A SURVIVORS GUIDE FOR GRIEF

~ Illustrated by my life, my experiences, and my photography

Grief

Sucks

Globally in 2020

JOHN & MARLISE PARTILLA

Table of Contents

LOVE, LIFE, HEART, MIND AND CAREERS ARE FRAGILE. THEY SHOULD NEVER BE TAKEN FOR GRANTED

— John S. Partilla

From the beginning, nature has survived. All of us have, at various times, had the opportunity to witness its strength and beauty. Now a father traveling with grief over the death of his son utilizes nature, his camera and his fountain pen as a way to survive.

I dedicate this garden to Jason, Brian, Joe, Corrie, Ian, Marlise, George, Laura, Jeff, Sean, Fraser, Justin, Jim, Frank, Grosi, David, Denny, Carl, JDawg, Arlene, Mike and THE COMPASSIONATE FRIENDS groups all over the world. A special acknowledgement to Fred Wineman who has helped so many.

We must go to school for learning the basics of life, but the topic of grief and death is not taught to the young. Please let me help you with this subject.

LIST OF MY REQUIRED SURVIVAL GEAR memories, survivors guide, camera, pen, hat, safe place to walk, walking stick, clear mind, tennis ball and good walking shoes.

"No Matter how dark it is where you stand, there is and always will be daylight somewhere in this universe. Please enjoy the day and the night."

— John S. Partilla

Prologue

The past is history, the future a mystery, today is a gift. That is why it is called a Present.

This is a powerful statement for any one who may be dealing with grief. Battling grief can be compared to battling terrorism. It is always with us.

Fifty five years ago, an eighteen year old U.S. Marine who volunteered for Vietnam, learned how to survive if he or his comrades were wounded in battle. He had to remember three life saving steps: Stop the bleeding, protect the wound and treat for shock.

When our son Jason and his friends were killed by a drunk driver, his father, mother, brother, family and friends began to fight a never-ending war. I wrote my book at that time to help myself and hopefully others, but the challenges that everyone has had to deal with in 2020 compelled me to take another look at my book. In the last days of 2019, a world war was started and millions have been wounded due to the corona virus. Now in the fall of 2020, we are going into shock. We ask ourselves "When will it end? Will there ever be a normal again?". This seemed like the time to offer a slightly altered version of our book, although the original idea remains the same. Find comfort in our photographs, quotes, emotions and experiences and add your own feelings through journaling along this Road to Survive.

On September 1, 2020 at 2:45 pm eastern time, CNN reported the following: "Authorities in 214 countries and territories have confirmed about 25.6 million Covid-19 cases and 852,000 deaths since China reported its first case to the World Health Organization (W.H.O.)". Every single one of these statistics reflects the mind, heart, emotions, feelings, friends and extended families of a real person and the numbers are growing by the minute. This virus does not care about time, age, country, gender, race, color, beliefs, religion or political party. Covid -19 immediately puts you on a Road To Survive with no real map or protection.

So that Marine is looking back to those three life savings steps from 55 years ago because we have all been wounded.

1. Stop the bleeding by wearing a mask, keeping a social distance and seeking help from friends or professionals.

2. Protect the wound by showing empathy, by caring and by communicating.

3. Treat for shock by using our book through journaling and sharing.

From our heart to your heart .
John and Marlise Partilla
www.griefsucks.net

"WE LIVE TO LOSE THE ONES WE LOVE" – John S. Partilla

MAY YOU CONTINUE TO SEEK KNOWLEDGE ABOUT GRIEF AND SHARE WHAT YOU HAVE LEARNED WITH OTHERS.

"ALWAYS LIVE FOR TODAY" - John S. Partilla

Our Family at McConnell's Mill, PA

Chapter one — Friends

Thank God for friends! They will show up, they will listen, they are your foundation in helping you through grief. Talk to them and support them because they may also need help. Let them "do their thing". Do not feel guilty about letting them into your home while you nap, cry or when you just need to escape from the outside world. Being alone is bad enough, but to be completely alone is terrible! Let them know if you want them to leave when you need that special moment of peace, but always be kind. Grief often brings out the wasted emotion of anger that you must learn to control.

Long after that terrible Day-One that has changed your life forever, you will need their help. The sooner you accept help for yourself, the sooner you can help others through your own experience. Try to use the phone, text, or send an email because others are worried about you. Accept a cup of coffee or a bite to eat. You must eat to maintain your strength. Go for a walk, but *please be aware of your surroundings*. You are no longer "playing with a full deck of cards", so be alert to everything. You do not want to get hurt or hurt someone else. Let your friends be your crutch.

Silence with a friend is sometimes as good as conversation. Ask for their help or for their opinion in making small decisions because you cannot do it all yourself.

Tell them how much they have helped you and write them a note. **Remember, everyone experiences grief** and you may have to help them one day. Be kind and appreciate your friends. They are a rock to stand on, a wall or tree to lean against and deserve the name of **FRIEND.**

I want to thank Bob, Barb, JoAnne, Mitch, John, Barb, Mike, Becky, Joe, Corey, Lee, Paul, Ted, Jeff, Cheryl, Marietta, Margie, Marlise, Ian, Dick, Ed, Denny, Glenn, Dave, Brad, Pat, Jason, Brian, Megan and Fred for treating my wounds.

"I NEVER QUESTIONED MY BLESSING'S, SO WHY SHOULD I QUESTION MY TRIALS" - (From the TV show "Sisters")

NOW IT IS YOUR TURN TO LIST THE FRIENDS

2

NAMES YOU CAN COUNT ON

Name, telephone, address

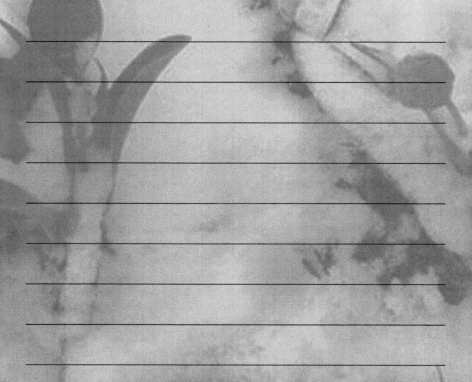

_____

_____

_____

_____

_____

_____

_____

_____

Chapter two — Family

Do not look for them to be your biggest support because they are suffering their grief also. On the other hand, they are your anchors in the storm. They know all the family problems and personality traits. Their grief is greater than you will ever know, but sometimes it will not show. Overlook the "God works in mysterious ways", "God doesn't give you anything you cannot handle" and last but not least, "time heals all". If that is what they believe or all that they are capable of offering, just listen and try not to get angry. Your family is no different than anyone else in not knowing what to say or when to be quiet. Fathers grieve differently than mothers; brothers differently than sisters, aunts than uncles, cousins than grandparents. **All you have to remember is everyone grieves differently.** I really believe that brothers and sisters have it harder than the parents. They hear "take care of your parents, be strong for them, they need you more than ever". Wow, that is tough on anyone let alone the brothers and sisters who are struggling with their own grief.

From my experience, I feel that my younger son, Ian, is the strongest of the family in dealing with grief, but only he knows how he really feels. My only wish for him is that he never gives up on his faith, family, friends and himself.

After 45 years of marriage, my wife is my best friend but I see how different her grief is compared to mine. We are often at completely different stages. We just try to remember to be patient with each other. Always go the extra mile, spend the extra time, go on vacations, take pictures, *laugh*, reminisce and cry when you need to. Parents must lead by example. Never send children anywhere without a smile and a hug! I have no regrets because I was a good father and friend to my kids. I took the time. My family came before work and also before myself.

I am grateful for my memories. *And I am grateful for my family!*

"LIFE ISN'T THE WAY IT'S SUPPOSED TO BE. LIFE IS THE WAY IT IS! IT'S HOW WE COPE THAT MAKES THE DIFFERENCE!" (From the TV show "Sisters")

IT IS YOUR TURN AGAIN TO LIST THE FAMILY YOU CAN COUNT ON!

Name, telephone, address

_____

_____

_____

_____

_____

_____

_____

_____

Chapter three — Reading

My friend Bob gave me my first book on grieving when his father died. I skimmed it for something to do on a summer night, not knowing what was in store for me during the next few months, and for the rest of my life. When Jason died, I grabbed the book frantically looking for an answer to Jason's tragic death and I found **NONE.**

What I did find was that *I was not alone.* Many others had experienced what I was going through, and though it was hard for me to believe, some had even experienced worse. I needed a road map to prepare me for this unplanned trip to Hell and back.

Surprisingly, I found that the first aid training I learned in the United States Marines was very helpful. First stop the bleeding, then protect the wound and finally treat for shock until professional medical help arrives. I followed this procedure then, and still do today. How do you stop the bleeding of grief? You don't. You just gradually learn to control it. You protect the wound through faith and going on. And you treat for shock through memories.

Along the road, I found challenging points that had never entered my mind. I learned how to deal with a trial, insurance companies, lawyers, potential health disorders for fathers, mothers, children.

I also found no mileposts for grief - only general stages and random times. Reading has become a lost pleasure, as has writing a letter. If your eyes can still focus through the tears and you have a quiet place to go, please read.

Remember you need support and comfort. If after reading an entire book, you have only highlighted one word or turned down one page corner, you have helped yourself and, hopefully, someone else down the road. Here are some suggestions of the books that have helped me.

by Betty J. Eddie

NOW ONCE AGAIN IT IS YOUR TURN TO LIST THE BOOKS, ARTICLES, OR WHATEVER YOU HAVE READ THAT HAS HELPED YOU IN THIS JOURNEY. REMEMBER THIS SAME LIST MIGHT BE THE FIRST-AID THAT HELPS SOMEONE ELSE!

_____

_____

_____

_____

_____

_____

_____

Chapter four — Memories

As you are reading this book, or any other book, use a favorite picture as a bookmark.

This is your chapter to write and read over and over again. Make it legible, start with dates, words, sentences and events. Have your favorite picture or flower next to you when you write. Print, write, make notes and let the memories flow. You are on your way to reading the best book ever written and you are writing it. Please share your story, feelings, and memories because we always need each other. We are all equal in grief and that is a universal fact. Tears are tears no matter which eyes they come from and no matter where on the earth they are falling.

GOOD LUCK AND START TO WRITE NOW!

_____

_____

_____

_____

_____

_____

_____

_____

_____

Chapter five — Tears

Let your tears flow, never be embarrassed and learn to be comfortable with them. Forget about others who do not understand, as long as you understand that tears are normal. Do not feel that you have to hide, but if you want a private moment to reflect, just excuse yourself. Many people, especially men, feel very uncomfortable when they cry. I think of the body as a pressure cooker that has a safety valve to let the steam out while cooking. Your body substitutes tears for steam and it lowers the stress while you are cooking mentally and physically. Crying, talking and hugging are all normal reactions, and will help you live with your grief. Hug a tree and hold on tight.

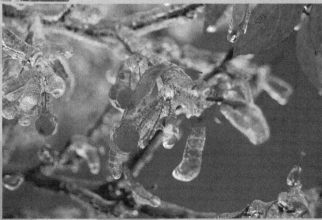

AGAIN IT IS YOUR TURN TO
WRITE ABOUT TEARS

_____

_____

_____

_____

_____

_____

_____

_____

_____

Chapter six — Music

No one can express the true feelings of grief better than musical artists. Their message comes through clearly and you can hear the message over and over again. Open your mind and their music will open your heart. Little by little your wound will start to feel better through their words and notes.

The following songs are special to me**:

- ☐ It's Not Easy Being Green

- ☐ Let It Be

- ☐ Cats in the Cradle

- ☐ Ghost Riders in the Sky

- ☐ I'll Keep Holding On

- ☐ My Favorite Things

- ☐ The Lonely Goat Herder (my wife is Swiss)

- ☐ The Sounds of Silence

- ☐ Tears in Heaven

- ☐ The Living Years

- ☐ It's So Hard to Say Good bye to Yesterday

- ☐ Theme from St. Elmo's fire

- ☐ You are the Sunshine of My Life

- ☐ Only the Good Die Young
- ☐ Coming to America
- ☐ That's What Friends Are For
- ☐ Some Days are Diamonds
- ☐ Country Roads (Jason went to West Virginia Univ)
- ☐ Rocky Mountain High (Ian went to Colorado State)
- ☐ Suddenly
- ☐ People are Strange
- ☐ Rocky Raccoon
- ☐ Over the Rainbow
- ☐ Theme from "Somewhere in Time"
- ☐ Evergreen
- ☐ Up Where We Belong
- ☐ Streets of Philadelphia
- ☐ You Don't Know What It's Like
- ☐ Reflections
- ☐ Forever Young
- ☐ Yesterday
- ☐ The Sound of Music
- ☐ Black Muddy River
- ☐ Box of Rain
- ☐ You Can't Always Get What You Want

- ☐ The Impossible Dream

- ☐ Day by Day

- ☐ Knock'n on Heaven's Door

- ☐ The Weight

- ☐ A Little Help from My Friends

- ☐ Fire and Rain

**Songwriters listed in Appendix*

18

IT IS YOUR TURN AGAIN TO LIST THE MUSIC THAT HELPS YOU!

_____

_____

_____

_____

_____

_____

_____

_____

_____

Chapter seven — The nine "f" words of grief

FIX – You cannot fix what has happened to you.

FIND – You will never find an answer.

FLOW – You must flow with life.

FAITH – You must have faith in living.

FEELINGS – You must never lose site of your feelings and those of others.

FRUSTRATING – Boy is it frustrating dealing with grief.

FRIENDS – You must trust them and be a friend to someone.

FOREVER – It is forever and very hard to accept.

FLOWERS – Plant them, touch them, take care of them and bring them into your life.

NOW IT IS YOUR TURN TO ADD TO THE LIST
OF WORDS THAT REFLECT TO YOUR GRIEF.

_____

_____

_____

_____

_____

_____

_____

_____

_____

Chapter eight — Reflections

I have listened, read, talked to others and made so many notes that I must share them with you! I cannot give the proper credits for the quotes but they come from very wise individuals. Some have experienced grief and some are just in tune to the needs of others. Remember it is what helps you, not me. Here is a list that I have heard over the last several years.

- ☐ Be kind and patient with yourself.

- ☐ Life is what is going on, while we are making plans.

- ☐ We were luckier than some and that is something to be satisfied with.

- ☐ If life is "so important" then why is it so fragile?

- ☐ Everyone wants to give us words of comfort but the trouble is ours.

- ☐ I think of him as just barely out of sight...just a few feet from my heart...just around the corner of wherever I happen to be on my path of life.

- ☐ It is up to us to heal.

- ☐ We must have hope!

- You are wrong, there **IS** something I can do about my grief.

- Quiet and nature are your best friend.

- May the force be with you.

- Not being able to bend is a danger, but bending like a tree prevents breaking.

- The measure of life after all is not its duration but its donation.

- If you hear his voice, harden not your heart.

- Do not give into grief, we care.

- You cannot predict life and you cannot change it. All you can do is live it.

- Anger is a wasted emotion and we must rise above it.

WHY? That's what we ask,
The truth is, we may never know for sure why
But we do know that there is no single
"should have done" or "did" or "didn't
do" that would have changed that why.
All that love could do was done.
- author unknov

- Thus the trick, the one big trick is to learn to try to understand it, but not question it.

- Who you are doesn't have anything to do with how long you are here, but whom you touch.

- A love that risks nothing is worth nothing.

- God shows us how to be strong, but we have to exercise.

- For who knows God's plans, or who can conceive what is intended for us. Who knows what time we are born or what time we leave. Don't worry, there are greater plans to be completed, gardens to be planted, flowers to be picked, and people to be helped.

- Life is full of unknown challenges that we must deal with.

- Holidays suck!

- Whether you live for an hour or one hundred years, life is still short.

- When you bury your parents you bury your past, when you bury your child you bury your dreams.

- God has given us the time so we do not have to rush.

- Something we fear the most is now here.

- God gives us the ingredients for our daily bread but we have to do the baking.

- Time and patience, little by little the acorn becomes a solid oak tree. Slowly we will again gain strength.

- The peace of a quiet landscape or garden nurtures us.

- Meditation can become an acceptable part of the healing. Powerful feelings of loss can only be healed by the warm powerful energy of the soul.

- We should admit that grief sucks, deal with it and seek help from others.

- Life is like a mountain range. There are sun-covered peaks you can never reach and right adjacent are valleys below the clouds that are so deep you cannot see the bottom. But look, the mountains start up from the darkness of the valleys and again are in the sun. Live and feel this image because this is life.

- The past is history, the future is a mystery and today is a gift that it is why we call it THE PRESENT.

- Never say for example "Jason had a great smile" always say, "Jason has a great smile". Learn from the "X" generation.

- Focus not with your mind but focus with your heart.

- Thank you for listening.

- Do not stand at my grave and weep, I am not there, I do not sleep, I am a thousand winds that blow, I am the diamond's gift on snow, I am the sunlight on ripened grain, I am the gentle Autumn rain. When you awaken in the morning's hush, I am the swift uplifting rush of quiet birds in circled flight. I am the soft stars that shine at night. Do not stand at my grave and cry, I am not there, I did not die.

- Open up, let the risk of life and sunshine in.

- Great sorrows are swept up into the vast love of the universe.

- Mountains are open, clean and filled with valleys and light.

- Never to have a clear picture of our selves or what is happening around us is too risky. In sharp focus we must find the beauty of life.

- A butterfly lights beside us like a sunbeam and for a brief moment its glory and beauty belong to our world. But then it flies on again, and though we wish it could have stayed, we feel so lucky to have seen it.

- Death is nothing at all. I have only slipped into the next room. Whatever we were to each other we still are.

- Call me by my old familiar name. Speak to me in the same easy way you always have. Laugh as we always laughed at the little jokes we enjoyed together. Play, smile, and think of me. Pray for me. Life means all that it ever meant. It is the same as it always was. There is an absolute unbroken continuity. Why should I be out of your mind because I am out of your sight? I am but waiting for you, for an interval, somewhere very near, just around the corner. All is well, nothing is past. Nothing has been lost. One brief moment, and all will be as it was before. Only better! Infinitely happier. We will be one, together forever.

- [ ] Enjoy the day, I hope it's sunny.

- [ ] Everybody says why me, I say why not me?

- [ ] He is your pilot, he will never take the wheel from your hands, but he will always give direction.

- [ ] Stay with me forever

- [ ] Grief comes like a violent storm and then you wait for the weather to clear.

- [ ] The only hard and scary part about falling in love is knowing that you must fight to hold onto it and never give up.

- [ ] Always remember the way they lived, not the way they died.

- [ ] It is not what you take with you when you leave this world, but what you leave.

- [ ] Life is not fair, but it was never promised to be.

IT IS YOUR TURN. WHAT ARE THE WORDS
THAT HELP AND THAT YOU WANT TO SHARE
WITH OTHERS? START LISTING THEM AND
REMEMBER TO WRITE OR PRINT LEGIBILY
SO THAT YOU CAN READ THEM LATER.

_____

_____

_____

_____

_____

_____

_____

Chapter nine — Movies

What can I say about movies is that they must make you feel good or DO NOT WATCH THEM. Turn the TV off it bothers you and only watch what helps. You have nothing to prove to anyone except to start healing! Here are the movies that help me and I watch them over and over again. Remember these are the ones that help me! Please list the ones that you would recommend.

- ☐ The Big Chill
- ☐ Moonstruck
- ☐ Soapdish
- ☐ The Godfather Part III
- ☐ Somewhere in Time
- ☐ Sleepless in Seattle
- ☐ The Majestic
- ☐ The Sound of Music
- ☐ Heaven can Wait
- ☐ The Return of the Dog Men
- ☐ Same Time Next Year
- ☐ Lost Boys
- ☐ Hawaii
- ☐ The Body
- ☐ Dying Young
- ☐ Millennium
- ☐ French Kiss
- ☐ Don Juan DeMarco
- ☐ Mr. Rice's Secret
- ☐ PS I love you

NOW IT IS YOUR TURN TO LIST THE MOVIES THAT HELP YOU!

_____

_____

_____

_____

_____

_____

_____

_____

_____

Chapter ten — Faith, signs, a place to go, and going on

You only have one option now and that is to keep going. Never give up, always have faith! Use all of your strength to find the good in yourself and the world. It is so easy to have a pity party but believe me, **no one will come except you**. Faith is like the foundation that the pyramids were built on. The pyramids have weathered the times and even though the outside of them are eroding, the foundations are still strong and solid. Although faith is a foundation for many, there are many others who struggle at this time. Why did God do this? How could God do this? You may be very angry with God for awhile. If you are, give yourself a break. If it lasts too long or affects your health, you may wish to seek professional help.

Signs are something that I have noticed and started talking about to others. Since the day my son died I have developed a sense for seeing, hearing and believing in a new dimension. Maybe I have just become more aware of life, but my senses have been sharpened. Several years ago, we were visiting our younger son, Ian, in Colorado. The morning we were leaving I was depressed and I turned on the TV to keep me company while I was waiting for the shuttle to the airport. A movie, "The Majestic", was playing. I started to watch and it was a story of a man whose son returned after being killed in World War II. He had been gone for 9 ½ years. This is how long Jason has been gone physically. Other things that weekend like butterflies, songs, visits to a hotel and a garden tour, all helped me maintain a tie with Jason. I believe even more that things are not just a coincidence! If you look you can find! We live in a world that is dimensionless and we must NOT define our own limits.

You must go on to help yourself and others. No one can be a better teacher than **YOU**!

Places to go that help me.

- Disney World for the laser show at Epcot
- A walk in the woods
- A walk in a botanical garden
- A walk on Lido beach in Sarasota, Florida
- Skiing in Squaw Valley, Vail, Breckenridge or Seven Springs
- A church on Sunday morning

"Bench at Coopers Rock Overlook"

- A cruise to St. Petersburg, Russia
- London
- My deck
- Niagara Falls
- McConnell's Mill
- Being alone
- Grindelwald Switzerland

"Compassionate Friends Memorial Garden "at Twin Lakes

NOW IT IS YOUR TURN TO LIST THE PLACES THAT GIVE YOU PEACE!

_____

_____

_____

_____

_____

_____

_____

_____

_____

_____

Chapter eleven — Lessons learned after 15 years

November 20, 2008

Today it has been exactly 15 years since Jason was killed by a drunk driver on November 20, 1993. I have decided to write chapter 11 and reprint my book for the second time. Here are additional reasons other than just this point in time.

1. It is the right thing to do for others.

2. I must thank so many people for standing by Marlise, Ian and me.

3. I must share my experience with all people who are going through grief and those who will go through grief in the future.

4. I must leave a memory of Jason in the minds of his niece Jorah and his young cousins Xavier, Matthew and Sarah. (note 2011: we have added another grand daughter Shaina and another cousin Anna)

5. It is the right thing to do for me!

Learning to cope #1

These are the priorities that I try to live by. It may help you to set your own priorities.

First — My faith in God. You may have your own form of faith.

Second — My wife who has also been my friend for over 40 years.

Third — My son Ian, Meagan, Jorah, Shaina and our extended families.

Fourth — My work.

Learning to cope #2

After 15 years in grief, the **HOLE** is still in my heart but I recently realized I can continue to love my wife, smile, laugh and live for another day.

Learning to cope #3

My wife and I always wear a butterfly pin on our clothing when we leave the house. We also wear a locket around our neck with the pictures of both of our sons inside. Ian has a tattoo of a butterfly but Marlise and I are afraid of the pain and the process, so we settled for the pin. You might consider getting a butterfly pin or locket because it can help. Remember everyone handles grief differently so there may be other items or options that will help you.

Learning to cope #4

I carry a small bubble level (used for hanging pictures) in my pocket with the word grief printed on the side. When I have a bad moment, I take it out and set it on a table to see that the bubble centers **IMMEDIATELY**. I then pick it up and attempt to center the bubble while holding it in my hand. It is very difficult and takes a steady hand, mind and body. It gives me a perspective on how easy it is for **LIFE TO GET OUT OF BALANCE**. You may want to add this small tool to your tool box and learn how to use it. **Remember you have a reason for feeling off balance.**

Learning to cope #5

After all of these years it has become even more important for me to talk about Jason but it still hurts and I miss him very much. I realize that it is a normal way for me to feel but a movie I saw helped to clarify the word "normal" for me. The movie is "Tombstone" starring Val Kilmer as Doc Holiday and Kurt Russel as Wyatt Earp. Near the end of the movie Doc Holiday is dying from a lung disease in Colorado. Wyatt Earp comes to visit Doc before his death and to play cards. Doc tells Wyatt what he wanted out of life. Then Doc says to Wyatt, "Wyatt what do you want?" Wyatt answers "Just to live a normal life." Doc says "There is no normal life Wyatt, there's just life, Now get on with it!" Think about this movie quote and realize how many others are feeling just like you. You are not the only one to be experiencing what you are experiencing and there will be many more every day. You must never give up, continue to live, help others and learn about life.

Learning to cope #6

No one called to talk to me today about Jason. I even forgot about the anniversary until Marlise asked me "What are we going to do today?" Jason always loved to decorate for Christmas, so we put up two trees and even went shopping. Every thing went fine until I started hearing the Christmas music and started feeling sorry for myself. Maybe next year I will be better but for now I still struggle with holidays. Try to prepare for the holidays, do what you can do and be satisfied with what you have accomplished. Also if you know of a person going through what you are, give them a call. It will probably help both of you.

Learning to cope #7

Thank you is a powerful word that is not said enough or taken seriously enough by people. I want to say **THANK YOU** to so many who have cared about Marlise, Ian and me. You know who you are so please remember that I am here for you also. May we always continue to share what we have to share with each other. Meagan, Jorah and Shaina thank you for coming into our lives.

Learning to cope #8

Over the last few years, I have found that I am much more tuned in to the lyrics in songs and the dialogue in movies and TV. After watching performances by Jim Morrison and Eric Clapton on TV, I recently started to read the lyrics of songs that have caught my attention. I think that I am always looking for a message or a lesson and the Band, the Grateful Dead, the Rolling Stones, the Beatles, and James Taylor among others, seem to express these messages to me. I often turn down the sound and use closed captioning if I really want to focus on the words being spoken or sung. It's amazing how much more I get out of reading and hearing at the same time.

Music has helped me a great deal and as a result I have created a CD with ten songs that I bought from the internet. This CD has often helped me in my grief and I listen to it over and over. Perhaps you can assemble your own special library of songs that may help you on those dark days. It may offer you some comfort as well.

Learning to cope #9

My book works for me and **Grief Does Suck!** Some people are offended by this term and have asked me to change the title and omit this word. I was even denied the opportunity to teach a grief support class at a Community College because the curriculum advisors said that "our students might be offended". Give me a break! Ask my son Ian if the word is appropriate or others who have lost a brother or sister! Ask any parent who has lost a child.

I remember a book signing I had at the Hilton Hotel in Pittsburgh when a woman grief counselor came up to me and said "Are you the author of Grief Sucks?" I cautiously said "Yes and I am sorry if I offended you." She replied "It is about time we have a word that really expresses what grief feels like for young adults."

I apologize if the term offends you, but I stand by it and so do many others who are grieving.

Learning to cope #10

During these last 8 years since I originally wrote this book, we have had three major joyful events that have made a significant difference in our lives. Ian met a wonderful young woman, Meagan. I can truthfully say that on the day they were married, I was truly happy. I know that Jason was there with us even though he was not there physically as best man. Ironically, Ian's friend, Jason was best man.

The other amazing events were the births of our grand daughters Jorah and Shaina. The J in Jorah is in memory of Jason. It really is true that it is possible to feel real happiness again. Life goes on and we will try to live it to the best of our ability.

I hope you can find SOMETHING in this short survivor's guide for grief. If you do, please share it with others and me. My email address is:

johnpartilla@ymail.com

From your friend in grief with respect, compassion and sincerity, John S. Partilla, father of Jason and Ian Partilla

Here is my picture that I call "Angel in the mountain sky". Can you see the angel?

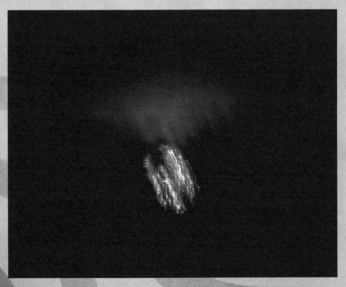

NOW IT IS YOUR TURN TO LIST THE THINGS THAT HELP YOU COPE!

_____

_____

_____

_____

_____

_____

_____

_____

_____

_____

Jason Scott Partilla

DECEMBER 19, 1972 – NOVEMBER 20, 1993

"Hi guys, just an update on the continuing adventure of me. Cape Cod was cool, we cruised in a convertible, saw whales, it was great! Next Rocky Horror Picture Show at Harvard. Later, Jason."

Thank you

As I go through grief, minute by minute, for the rest of my life over the loss of my son, I realize I am not alone. There is help. Jason lived, loved his life, his family, his friends and the environment.

Since Jason's death, I have worn a small butterfly every day to work and play. I want all who grieve, or will someday grieve, to know that grief is normal, and life in this world is not forever. Life is fragile and can change in a <u>second of time</u>, as it did for our family and friends. We can see the beauty and donation that a fragile butterfly contributes to nature and to us in its short lifetime. Our children are like butterflies. We must not focus on the duration of time we shared with them. We must focus on a smile, a memory, a moment of happiness they have donated to our hearts.

Visit my website at <u>www.griefsucks.net</u>

John S. Partilla

APPENDIX

- [ ] It's Not Easy Being Green - Joe Rapozo

- [ ] Let It Be - John Lennon and Paul McCartney

- [ ] Cats in the Cradle – Harry Chapin

- [ ] Ghost Riders in the Sky – Stan Jones

- [ ] I'll Keep Holding On – Ivy Jo Hunter

- [ ] My Favorite Things – Rodgers and Hammerstein

- [ ] The Lonely Goat Herder – Rodgers and Hammerstein

- [ ] The Sounds of Silence – Paul Simon

- [ ] Tears in Heaven – Eric Clapton and Will Jennings

- [ ] The Living Years – Mike Rutherford and B.A. Robertson

- [ ] It's So Hard to Say Good bye to Yesterday – Freddie Perren and Christine Yarian

- [ ] Theme from St. Elmo's fire – David Foster

- [ ] You are the Sunshine of my Life – Stevie Wonder

- [ ] Only the Good Die Young – Billy Joel

- [ ] Coming to America – Neil Diamond

- [ ] That's What Friends Are For – Carole Bayer Sager & Burt Bacharach

- [ ] Some Days are Diamonds – Dick Feller

- [ ] Country Roads – Bill Danoff and Taffy Nivert

- Rocky Mountain High – Michael Taylor and John Denver

- Suddenly – John Farrar

- People are Strange – Jim Morrison, John Densmore, Robbie Krieger and Ray Mazarek

- Rocky Raccoon – John Lennon and Paul McCartney

- Over the Rainbow – E.Y. Harburg and Harold Arlen

- Theme from "Somewhere in Time"–Rachmaninoff

- Evergreen – Paul Williams and Barbara Streisand

- Up Where We Belong – Will Jennings

- Streets of Philadelphia – Bruce Springstein

"Can you feel her tears?"

- [ ] You Don't Know What It's Like - David Gates

- [ ] Reflections – Lamont Dozier

- [ ] Forever Young – Rod Stewart, Jim Cregan, Kevin Savigar and Bob Dylan

- [ ] Yesterday – Paul McCartney and John Lennon

- [ ] The Sound of Music – Rodgers and Hammerstein

- [ ] Black Muddy River – Jerry Garcia and Robert Hunter

- [ ] Box of Rain – Robert Hunter and Phil Lesh

- [ ] You Can't Always Get What You Want – Mick Jagger and Keith Richards

- [ ] The Impossible Dream – Joe Darion and Mitch Leigh

- [ ] Day by Day – Stephen Schwartz

- [ ] Knock'n on Heaven's Door – Bob Dylan

- [ ] The Weight – Robbie Robertson

- [ ] With a Little Help from My Friends – Paul McCartney and John Lennon

- [ ] Fire and Rain – James Taylor

Chapter Twelve — Grief still sucks after 20 years

November 20, 1993 to November 20, 2013

Good morning, it is 3:00 AM and I cannot sleep. My mind is racing and I feel the "Force" again driving me to share my thoughts and feelings. Living with this disability called grief for the past 20 years has been difficult, confusing and challenging. In my mind I have changed so much and sometimes it scares me.

One thing that I know for sure is GRIEF STILL SUCKS! I cannot find a better or more clinical word to describe these ongoing feelings. I did not want to be a Father In Grief (FIG) but I have started using the acronym in my writing. I am sure that neither my wife nor my son wants to be a mother in grief or brother in grief but they have no option.

Many wonderful and some difficult events have happened to me since I wrote CHAPTER ELEVEN – LESSONS LEARNED AFTER 15 YEARS. We have two wonderful granddaughters. We have relocated to Denver. Our health is good. We have amazing opportunities for travel. We have been able to celebrate 45 years of marriage. We had a Partilla family reunion in Disney World and in addition we have celebrated with our family and friends for weddings, births, graduations and engagements. I am also grateful to be able to share my grief and to support others who are in need. There is no reason to list the difficult things because as I have said in the past we must focus on good memories not bad memories or difficult times.

Probably the most positive thing has been that my faith in the future has grown stronger. Once again it is my foundation. The first job I had after the Marine Corps and school was working for a USS railroad company. I still look at many things through the eyes of that young draftsman/surveyor and engineer. I see my foundation of faith both symbolically and physically. Nothing can stand the storm of life without a foundation properly designed and tested. The ongoing test is difficult. It is like designing a bridge or a structure to withstand an earthquake or a flood. The design is always for the worst flood or strongest earthquake possible for the location you need to build. A safety factor is then added and the structure is built. There is no guarantee the new bridge will stand forever but all decisions are made based upon the facts that you know at the time, with the chance the storm, flood or earthquake can be larger in the future. You must be ready to frequently maintain, inspect and evaluate the bridge so that it is strong enough to support the heavy loaded cars that the engine is pulling. You will always need to invest time, energy and money to redesign and reinforce as required. Then for all future structures you must move forward with new criteria, being diligent about potential ongoing changes needed to have a safe bridge or building. Sometimes you may not have to strengthen but just perform good ongoing maintenance.

Just as steam locomotives pound and hammer the bridges, grief can pound and hammer a person down, often deteriorating both mental and physical health. How can I compare this to my faith? My faith in the future makes me willing to inspect, listen and maintain my mind and body to survive in this very challenging environment that I live in. My faith keeps me going in times when I might want to give up and let the bridge fall. The loaded cars I must pull are burdened with grief and they will not get lighter. So I must get stronger and smarter. It takes hard work and flexibility. It takes listening to my partner, letting my friends help, even finding new friends who never knew Jason. I must be willing to change, to share, to give back, to be aware of others in need, to find new ways to help myself when needed. The best way I can honor my son is to continue to have the faith that will help me to "Always look at the bright side of life"!

(A song that Jason liked from Monty Python)

Epilogue — Grief really sucks in 2020

It is still hard to accept that we have not hugged, kissed or talked to our son Jason in 27 years! So many things have changed and have happened to us that continue to pull the scabs of grief from the permanent holes in our hearts. The raw wound begins to bleed and then once again slowly starts to heal. We are not alone because this process is normal and occurs daily for many others.

We think these days of all that has occurred for our family without the physical presence of Jason. We watch our grand daughters, Jorah and Shaina, as they laugh, swim, paint, ski and grow to be independent young women. Uncle Jason would have loved joining us on our trip exploring Switzerland and visiting cousins. So as we deal with our loss, we think of all of those who are experiencing their own loss <u>especially at this time</u> and we continue to reach out to help others

<u>Especially at this time</u>. There have been other events that have impacted the entire world including other pandemics and wars. Because this pandemic feels a little like World War 3, I have been thinking of the comparison to World War 2 when families were separated for years or forever, the news of deaths were delivered by telegrams, and the full impact was not understood until months and years later. Today through technology, the grief is live, instantaneous, twenty four hours a day. Millions of new victims are grieving everyday as families and friends are separated through illness and the fear of illness. The worry of never seeing someone again is all tied up to grief as we travel on a Road to Survive.

So we must find our faith and never lose it. Our minister Rev. Kevin Maly expressed this so well in his benediction every Sunday.

"Go forth into the world in peace.
Be of good courage.
Hold fast that which is good.
Render to no one evil for evil.
Strengthen the faint hearted.
Support the weak.
Help the afflicted.
Honor all people.
The blessing of God, the father rest upon you this day and remain with you forevermore".

Wishing everyone peace and the strength to deal with all the changes in your life.

Please never give in to grief. You must make the decision to survive against all odds using hope and faith as your foundation to build upon.

Please look forward to the light of 2021 but never forgetting 2020 and its darkness.

Once again, from our heart to your heart

John and Marlise Partilla

With respect John and Marlise Partilla

IT IS NOW YOUR TURN TO WRITE THE LESSONS YOU HAVE LEARNED!

_____

_____

_____

_____

_____

_____

_____

_____

_____

_____